i

Adam and Eve Were Chinese

How Population Math and Ancient Clues Point to an Eastern Genesis

"Maybe the Garden of Eden was planted in Chinese soil after all.
But could it have been because apple trees just grow better there?"

— *A provocative theory on the origins of humanity and its myths*

First Edition
Published in the United States of America
ISBN: [979-8-9987839-1-3]

~ Dedication ~

To the restless minds – the questioners, the quiet rebels, the ones who look at the stars and wonder *if we've gotten the story all wrong.*

To the ancient ones whose voices echo through stone and myth, and to the future ones who will rewrite everything we thought we knew.

And to those who stood beside me – in conversation, in silence and in support, whether you realized it or not.

Your presence – in body and in spirit – helped this book take form!

JS

Table of Contents

"If it wasn't the chicken that came first, and if it wasn't the egg that came first, then it must have been the rooster who came first."

— *From the Stardust Chronicles*

Before the hen and the egg, there was the rooster – standing at the dawn of creation.

Introduction

Where we came from is not just a question of ancient history, it's a question of identity. Human origin stories have shaped our philosophies, our politics, our religions, and even our sense of purpose. And yet, for all our advances in science, genetics, and archaeology, the story of humanity's true beginning remains, at best, a work in progress.

The most widely accepted model for human origin, called the *Out-of-Africa* theory, proposes that all anatomically modern humans, or *Homo sapiens*, originated in Africa around 200,000 years ago and gradually migrated outward to populate the rest of the world. This view is supported by fossil evidence, mitochondrial DNA, and scientific consensus. It is taught in schools, referenced in documentaries, and cited as settled fact in countless publications.

But consensus is not the same thing as proof. And as with any theory, especially one with such sweeping historical and philosophical implications, it deserves periodic reevaluation.

This short work offers an alternate possibility: that the first truly modern human pair, or what we might symbolically refer to as *Adam and Eve*, originated not in Africa, but in East Asia, most likely in what is now China. This hypothesis is not built on theology, nationalism, or any religious ideology, but rather is built on a simple question of demographic logic: If one population group now comprises a staggering share of the global population count, could that be evidence that their lineage began earlier than we thought?

The Chinese people currently represent nearly one in every six humans alive on Earth. This is not a trivial number. If we group the world's national populations into roughly 200 categories of our species (also called "nationalities"), the Chinese represent one out of one hundred and ninety, but where they account for more than 17% of the total. That imbalance is mathematically startling and begs to be examined not as coincidence, but possibly as a signal that challenges how we interpret long-term human history.

While genetics has helped clarify our shared ancestry, it has yet to fully explain something far more visible and immediate: the extraordinary anatomical and phenotypic diversity across the human race. From the tightly coiled hair of Sub-Saharan Africans to the epicanthic folds of East Asians, from the broad stature of Polynesians to the pale freckled skin of Northern Europeans, these differences are not subtle, nor are they easily explained by sunlight exposure and migration alone. They hint at a deeper mystery, one that may require a more layered view, even a more *parallel layered* view, of how humanity first emerged and then diversified in nature.

This book is not about trying to disprove evolution; and its focus or scope is not concerned with any religious order trying to prove or disprove the Holy Bible. Similarly, it is not an attempt to elevate one culture or identity above another, whether physically or ideologically. Indeed, it is a thought experiment, or a data-driven, symbolic exploration of whether our current understanding of humanity's origin may have blind spots.

You won't find absolute answers here. What you will find is an invitation to think more deeply, as well as more numerically, about where we came from. In this way, we will be exploring a conceptual term that the author of this work has coined – the *Genesis Effect.* And maybe – just maybe – you'll leave with the sense that the oldest story ever told still has more pages left to turn.

Every journey begins with a single step across an unseen threshold.

Chapter 1: The Out-of-Africa Paradigm

In modern anthropology and genetics, one theory has stood taller than the rest when it comes to explaining the origin of Homo sapiens: the *Out-of-Africa* model.

It is taught in schools, cited in academic journals, and widely accepted in scientific and public discourse. According to this view, all modern humans share a common origin in Africa, from which they migrated and populated the rest of the world.

The theory, as it stands today, suggests that anatomically modern humans evolved in East Africa between 200,000 and 300,000 years ago. From there, small populations began migrating northward and eastward; first into the Middle East, then Asia, and eventually across the globe. By this model's standards, every human alive today descends from a relatively small African population that left the continent approximately 60,000 to 70,000 years ago.

The Out-of-Africa model is built on three primary pillars: fossil records, genetic data, and the analysis of mitochondrial DNA (mtDNA).

Fossils of early Homo sapiens found in places like Omo Kibish, and Jebel Irhoud in Africa, date back as far as 300,000 years. These discoveries helped establish Africa as the presumed cradle of modern human life.

Studies of genetics, particularly those examining mitochondrial DNA (passed only through mothers), have shown that African populations exhibit the greatest genetic diversity, which is a trait that evolutionary biologists interpret as a marker of ancestral origin.

Additionally, the Y-chromosome data and autosomal DNA studies point to a common African lineage before populations diversified and adapted across the planet.

While the Out-of-Africa model was once a bold hypothesis competing with others, such as the now largely discarded Multiregional Continuity model, it gained traction through the late 20th century as new tools in genetics became widely available. The mapping of the human genome, combined with radiocarbon dating and increasingly sophisticated DNA extraction techniques, gave researchers new confidence in tracing the human family tree.

By the early 2000s, the theory had moved from hypothesis to paradigm, a lens through which most human origin studies were viewed. Museum exhibits, documentaries, and school curricula all began to align with this new consensus. The idea that *"we are all African"* became both a scientific message and, increasingly, a political or cultural one emphasizing unity, shared ancestry, and the common humanity of all people. (NOTE: Some critics have noted that the phrase, "we are all African," while promoting unity, may unintentionally oversimplify human diversity and suppress alternate theories of parallel emergence.)

The Out-of-Africa model is elegant in its simplicity. It explains:

• Why genetic diversity is greatest in Africa: Older lineages have had more time to accumulate variation.

• Why fossil evidence of archaic humans is abundant in Africa: The region's geography and climate may have supported early hominid evolution.

• How different human populations share the common traits of migration, adaptation, and interbreeding with archaic humans (like Neanderthals and Denisovans) helps to explain global diversity without requiring separate origin points.

It also promotes a unifying narrative: that all humans, regardless of race, culture, or geography, ultimately share a single ancestral homeland.

Despite its strengths, the Out-of-Africa model is not without unresolved questions.

Fossil finds in China, the Middle East, and even Europe suggest that Homo sapiens, or pre-sapiens ancestors, may have been present outside of Africa earlier than expected.

The genetic timelines don't always match the fossil record, leading to debates about whether human evolution was a single origin event or a mosaic of overlapping migrations and adaptations.

The model often simplifies complex population dynamics into a neat linear narrative. Real migration was likely far messier, with back-migrations, regional isolation, and crossbreeding shaping our species in ways we are only beginning to understand.

And then there's the demographic reality: a massive and seemingly disproportionate rise of one population group - the Chinese - who today represent nearly a fifth of the human race. If all Homo sapiens started from the same genetic bottleneck, then why did one lineage flourish more explosively than all the others? Could there be something deeper, perhaps even earlier, going on beneath the assumptions?

That question leads us to the next chapter, where we begin to explore the demographic imbalance that lies at the heart of the *Out-of-China* hypothesis, which is the primary focus of this thought experiment.

Did the dawn of man truly rise from the West, or was it from the East?

Chapter 2: The Demographic Imbalance

At the time of this writing, the global human population hovers just above eight billion. It's a number so vast it resists imagination, yet one simple fact stands out among the data: more than 1.4 billion of those people are Chinese, which in itself is a vast number. That means roughly one in every six humans on Earth belongs to a single nationality, of which there are approximately 200 nationalities; and it is an imbalance unlike anything else in the human demographic landscape.

This isn't a cultural judgment, and it certainly isn't a nationalist commentary. It's a factual statistical anomaly, a standout figure that begs to be examined, if not explained. Because if we assume that all modern humans evolved from a single common population relatively recently, as the Out-of-Africa theory proposes, then why did one group – and only one – expand so dramatically beyond the rest?

If we loosely group global populations by distinct national or ethnic identities, say 190 to 200 distinct population branches (i.e., analogous to how we classify hundreds or thousands of breeds among canines, felines, birds and so forth), the Chinese represent just one of those groups. And yet, that one group makes up over 17% of the global population.

That's more than just disproportionate. That's algebraically bold.

If all of humanity emerged from a common ancestral stock 60,000 to 100,000 years ago, and if genetic diversification occurred through climate, migration, and random drift, shouldn't we expect a more even distribution of population branches? Shouldn't a single origin, a single root system, result in a fairly balanced outgrowth of cultural and physical branches over time?

But that's not what we see. Instead, we find one branch exploding while most others plateau or remain steady and relatively small.

This isn't about superiority. It's about asking an uncomfortable, data-driven question: Could this extreme demographic imbalance be evidence of something deeper, perhaps an earlier origin, or a different origin altogether?

The dominant evolutionary model treats human development like a single tree trunk, splitting into branches over time as people migrated and adapted. This is a useful metaphor, but really only until you start comparing it to other trees in the broader spectrum of life throughout the Earth.

Because here's what you don't see in nature: a single lineage producing the kind of sweeping anatomical, cultural, and genetic divergence found in humans, and all within just a few thousand generations. There's no clear precedent for it ever happening with any other species of animal. Not in wolves. Not in birds. Not in anything. And yet, in the case of Homo sapiens, that's exactly what the Out-of-Africa model expects us to accept.

People with skin as dark as obsidian and as pale as snow, people with hair textures as tight as springs and as straight as silk, people with body types ranging from the slight frames of Southeast Asia to the broad-shouldered might of Pacific Islanders, with all supposedly emerging from a common source or group, both relatively recently and through little more than climate and sunlight exposure.

It's not that this is necessarily impossible, but instead that it's mathematically and biologically uncomfortable, or even unlikely. And honestly, even saying that is just a courtesy, a way of giving the benefit of the doubt for its own sake. Because like I say, there's no clear precedent for it happening anywhere else in nature. (<u>NOTE</u>: This question is covered in the **Reader Q&A** section of this book.)

The Chinese population didn't gradually grow into dominance through colonial expansion or political conquest, unlike say the Roman Empire did. Their numerical strength has been consistent over centuries, even millennia, according to historical records. Despite wars, famines, dynastic shifts, and more, the sheer size of this population has remained a constant feature of the human world map.

If we look at that fact not just as a coincidence, but as evidence, it suggests one of two things:

1. Chinese were the first to emerge, and thus had a head start; or

2. They evolved separately, through an origin point that paralleled, rather than followed, the African one. In other words, the emergence of the African people would have been one Genesis Effect, while the emergence of the Chinese people would have been a separate, or parallel, Genesis Effect, and regardless of which came first.

Either possibility threatens to collapse the simplicity of the single-tree model.

What if, instead of one tree, humanity is more like a forest? What if nature did what it seems to do everywhere else, which is to generate similar forms through separate, localized starting points?

We see this with wolves, foxes, and dogs. We see it with tigers, leopards, and jaguars. We see it with species of birds, fish, and frogs that look similar but emerged independently in vastly different parts of the world.

Why would humans be the exception?

This chapter doesn't aim to prove anything. It aims to reframe a question. It's not enough to say, *"Well, the Chinese are numerous because they have a long agricultural history"* or that *"population grows with time and land."* That may be true, but it's not enough.

When one branch of the human family accounts for nearly 20% of all people alive, and no other group comes even close, it's not unreasonable to ask whether that branch started growing earlier, or separately, or both.

And once we start asking that question seriously, we may find that the old answers no longer hold up.

In the next chapter, we will explore what happens when you invert the paradigm entirely: when you ask not --"Where did we all come from?" but rather, "What if each of us came from somewhere different?"

— ✧ —

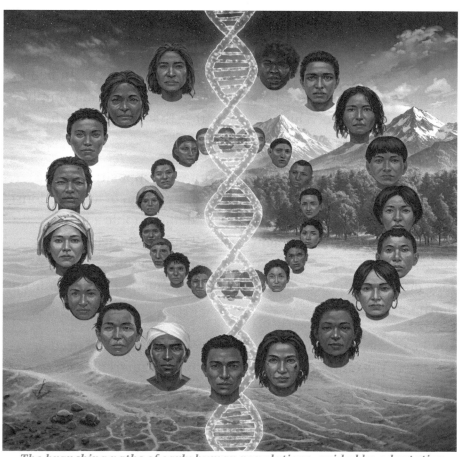

The branching paths of early human populations, guided by adaptation and migration.

Chapter 3: The Out-of-China Hypothesis

At some point, a theory becomes so deeply accepted that questioning it feels subversive. The idea that modern humans originated in Africa and then spread outward across the globe is one such theory; widely accepted, taught universally, and built on multiple layers of fossil and genetic evidence.

But as we saw in the previous chapter, the statistical dominance of one group – more than 1.4 billion Chinese – raises a compelling question: What if the dominant group on the planet isn't simply a successful branch of a human family tree that began elsewhere? What if they were the root?

The *Out-of-China Hypothesis* begins not with opposition to the African origin model, but with a simple inversion of assumptions: It asks whether China's extraordinary demographic and civilizational continuity might be more than historical coincidence. It suggests that the region known today as East Asia may not just be a receiver of human evolution and civilization, but a primary source.

Unlike many global populations that rose and fell, fractured or migrated, the Chinese civilization exhibits a remarkable sense of civilizational inertia; notably that it has remained rooted in the same region with continuous cultural, linguistic, and agricultural identity for thousands of years. This level of uninterrupted geographic and intellectual continuity is arguably unparalleled in world history.

China is not just populous, it is enduring. Dynasties have come and gone, emperors have risen and fallen, but the people remained, adapted, and carried their culture forward without a total reset. Few other societies can say the same.

One of the most striking historical moments that hints at China's global potential, and how it abruptly turned inward, comes from the early 15th century during the Ming Dynasty. At the time, under the leadership of Admiral Zheng He, China possessed the largest and most advanced navy in the world.

Zheng He's so-called *'Treasure Fleets'* embarked on massive voyages from 1405 to 1433. These expeditions were monumental: some ships stretched over 400 feet long, or nearly five times the length of Christopher Columbus's ships, which wouldn't cross the Atlantic for another 60 years. Zheng He commanded hundreds of vessels and tens of thousands of men, sailing to ports in Southeast Asia, India, Arabia, and even the east coast of Africa.

There is a provocative theory, explored in works like Gavin Menzies' book *'1421: The Year China Discovered America,'* that one or more of Zheng He's fleets may have reached the Americas before Columbus ever set sail. While this theory remains controversial and outside mainstream academic consensus, it underscores one fact beyond dispute: China had both the capacity and the knowledge to reach the farthest corners of the world centuries before Europe would dominate the seas.

And then, in an almost unthinkable move, China stopped. Under a new emperor, the Ming Dynasty ordered the ships destroyed, the shipyards dismantled, and all long-distance exploration banned. In one of history's most bewildering decisions, the world's most powerful navy was deliberately burned by its own command.

Why China chose to veer away so abruptly and decisively from its seemingly plotted course of being an expeditionist culture throughout much of its history remains an open question. And that question, while not really a focal point of this book's narrative, is an interesting side note to nonetheless consider.

Could it be that just as Earth matured beyond the Genesis Effect, perhaps China, too, had reached a civilizational apex and deliberately chose stillness over expansion? We're left to wonder – and perhaps accept – that the answer lies buried somewhere deep in China's ideological past.

However, this moment of inward retreat by China (whatever the reasons) may have changed the trajectory of world history. But perhaps it was not an aberration and was simply a flicker of something older – a brief reminder of a global presence that may have once been far more expansive than modern memory recalls.

The Out-of-China Hypothesis doesn't claim with certainty that Homo sapiens first emerged in East Asia, but it does ask why we so confidently assume they didn't. It argues that population dominance, civilizational longevity, and cultural coherence are signals worth reading, not anomalies to ignore.

And it asks us to question whether Homo sapiens spread out from a single origin, or emerged simultaneously – or sequentially – in more than one place.

Because when we look at the natural world, we do not see single-origin stories. We see parallel developments. We see ecosystems generating similar species through local conditions, not universal ancestry. No one claims that all canine species came from one dog, or that all frogs, all snakes, or all trees trace to a single pair. We accept parallelism as a mainstream and fundamental part of the story of life.

Why not for us?

In the next chapter, we'll follow that question through the lens of ancient texts, directional symbolism, and what it means to know how the biblical account of the Book of Genesis itself is seen placing the Garden of Eden – *'eastward in Eden.'* Perhaps the clues we've been ignoring have always pointed... east.

A symbolic glimpse of humanity's genesis — shaped by cosmic forces beyond time and geography.

Chapter 4: Rethinking the Genesis Effect - Ancient Clues & Symbolic East

Throughout history, the East has been more than a direction, it has been a symbol. In ancient texts, sacred mythologies, and classical cosmologies, the East is almost always depicted as the source, the origin and the place where light and life begin.

In the Book of Genesis, we are told not that Eden was placed in the West or the North, but that *'the Lord God planted a garden eastward in Eden,'* (as stated in Genesis 2:8). This phrasing is curious, almost poetic in its simplicity, but perhaps deeper in its meaning. Why emphasize the East at all? Why was it necessary to note specific direction?

To ancient peoples, cardinal direction wasn't just geography, it was theology, cosmology, and cultural philosophy. The East represented birth, renewal and illumination. The Sun rises in the East; the day begins in the East. Civilizations that arose earliest in history – Mesopotamia, India, China – were eastern in relation to the later centers of Western Europe.

The Bible's symbolic East reference might have originally pointed toward Mesopotamia or the Indus Valley; but in a broader reading, it could just as easily be interpreted as a metaphor for the lands far beyond, which are lands that, even by early historical standards, were already ancient. These are lands like China.

And here, once again, the demographic data aligns with ancient intuition: If the East is the direction of origin in myth, and if China is the most enduring and populous culture in that symbolic East, is it not at least plausible that the myth points toward something deeper? Could the ancient language of Genesis, perhaps unknowingly, have echoed a biological truth encoded in geography?

This chapter does not aim to repurpose sacred texts for secular science, nor to claim divine revelation as demographic proof. But it is worth taking note of how often humanity's oldest stories point to the East – not the West, nor the South – as the wellspring of life and mystery.

Even outside of scripture, the East has always held a kind of gravitational power in the human psyche. Chinese civilization developed some of the earliest known innovations in astronomy, medicine, paper, silk, and agriculture. Their philosophical systems, namely Confucianism, Taoism and Buddhism, arose long before Western institutions would lay claim to reason and law.

And unlike many ancient civilizations that crumbled or were overtaken, China remained. It persisted. It adapted without losing its memory. In a world of cultural churn and reset, China represents continuity, not just in population, but in consciousness as well.

Now consider what we touched on earlier: the relatively limited technological development of some other nationalities at the time of global contact. When European explorers reached the Americas in the 15th and 16th centuries, they encountered civilizations that had built pyramids and calendars, but also tribes who still lived in skin tents, rode horses as the primary mode of transportation, and hunted with flint-tipped arrows. North American Indigenous cultures, while deeply spiritual and ecologically attuned, had not developed metalworking, long-range navigation, or firearms.

Indeed, most (not all) also lacked masonry skills, such as mortar-based construction or use of quarried stone.

In Sub-Saharan Africa, much the same was true: While rich in oral traditions and regional empires, there was a noticeable absence of seafaring technology, industrial metallurgy, or large-scale written records by the time Europeans arrived. This is not a critique, but is an observation. These cultures may not have been 'lesser' in terms, but they may have been later to arrive on the scene.

If we imagine, even for a moment, that human nationalities emerged not from a single source, but from multiple parallel "Genesis Effects" in different regions of the world, then it would make perfect sense that some groups would appear earlier and others later. The variances in technological advancement may not reflect external oppression or internal deficiency – but simply sequence.

Under that framework, the East, and especially China, may have hosted the earliest spark. And that possibility, however controversial, aligns eerily well with the very philosophical stories we've been telling ourselves for thousands of years.

Maybe the *Garden* really was planted *'eastward in Eden.'* Maybe the myths we inherited carry more than metaphor: maybe they carry *memory*.

In the next chapter, we will return to the realm of logic and mathematics, building a case for why the numbers themselves seem to favor the model of multiple human emergences. Because when nature creates life, it rarely does so just once.

— ✦ —

The final spark: A barrier against spontaneous creation, locking Earth's biosphere into place.

Chapter 5: Rethinking Origin Through Numbers

Let's set aside symbolism for a moment and deal with the cold, rational world of numbers. Because if we want to talk about origins, about people, about populations, as well as about the vast patchwork of life on Earth, then math may tell a story that fossils and genetics alone do not.

At the time of this writing, there are more than eight billion people on Earth. That's a staggering number. But what's even more staggering is the uneven distribution of those people. The Chinese account for over 1.4 billion. Add in India and you're approaching 3 billion from just two nations. Then scatter the rest across 190 or so distinct nationalities, languages, and ethnic histories and you have the ingredients for some dynamic mathematical observations.

This isn't just about geography. It's a numerical clue. And when we reverse-engineer population dominance, we often find ourselves looking back toward something deeper: origin.

Now let's apply a simple mathematical concept to the question of human emergence: If we assume that Homo sapiens emerged from a single point, one small population that spread out over tens of thousands of years, then we should expect a fairly uniform distribution of genetic representation across the globe. But that's not what we see. What we see are enormous disparities in genetics.

Some nationalities remain in the hundreds of thousands. Others number in the hundreds of millions. One nationality, the Chinese, numbers over a billion. This makes the single-origin hypothesis feel strangely imbalanced. It suggests that all diversity and population variance sprouted from a lone event and that one branch just happened to explode while others did not. The odds of that scenario playing out randomly are statistically slim, even unlikely. And any responsible bookmaker – or *bookie* – wouldn't even entertain giving odds on such an enormously improbable outcome in view of a betting scenario, mainly because no responsible bettor would place such a bet.

But what if we stop thinking in terms of a singular origin and start thinking in terms of parallel emergence? What if, like trees in a forest, multiple human lineages began in different places, under different conditions, at different times – the same as we know happened with most other species?

That would explain the diversity. It would explain the imbalance. And it would also match what we see in the rest of nature, where closely related species often emerge independently of each other, as well as across vast distances, and subsequently adapt to their unique ecological conditions. Since all dog breeds, for example, belong to the broader canine species, an Alaskan Husky is uniquely adapted to harsh, freezing temperatures. Conversely, other canine breeds are best-suited to the *rolling plains*, or moderate climates, and could not survive extreme cold.

Then consider this: If these separate groups of humans did indeed emerge independently, each from a unique 'Genesis Effect' occurrence, why don't we see new human nationalities forming today?

With that question in mind, we introduce a critical concept: maturity. Not maturity just of individuals, but of ecosystems, of planetary biological systems, and of genesis origins themselves.

Every living thing has a growth phase. Trees reach a maximum height. Animals stop growing. Even stars, in their own way, experience birth, maturity, and burnout. What if the Earth's capacity to spark new life followed the same pattern?

In the early stages of Earth's biosphere, certain environmental, atmospheric, and energetic conditions may have been just right to foster the spontaneous emergence of life – possibly even complex life – in localized forms. These genesis events may have birthed the first fish, the first bird, the first serpent, the first frog. And yes, the first pair of humans – a male and female. One pair for each type, or breed. And then... nothing more. The cycle would have simply ended, or exhausted itself, as in reaching a growth plateau that is notably the rule in nature, not the exception. In this way, the concept of entropy – amounting to burnout – is a valid consideration to make.

Because like any mature organism, the Earth itself may have passed through its formative window. Once life was established and diversified enough to sustain itself through reproduction, the conditions that had made spontaneous genesis possible may have simply... expired.

We don't see mold endlessly forming on the top layer of tomato soup resting in a *petri dish*. We don't see forests producing new root systems once the canopy is complete. And we don't see humans continuing to emerge from the clay of the Earth, not because it never happened, but because the ecosystem no longer requires it, and – more importantly – would not be able to support it anyway in the same way that nature does not support organisms growing forever and forever into perpetuity.

This doesn't contradict science. It expands it. Evolution remains in play. Genetics still drive reproduction. But the origin of the types, the nationalities, the anatomies, the species, indeed the breeds themselves, may have occurred in one finite burst; or to have occurred as a planetary maturation process not unlike puberty or adolescence occurs. The argument is for a single cycle of biological seeding.

And once that seeding was complete, it stopped. Not because it failed, but because it succeeded. The seed was planted, it sprouted and grew, and then it stopped growing. That's how nature works.

In the next chapter, we'll step back from mathematics and return to myth. There, in the story of Noah's Ark, we'll find what may be the Bible's symbolic memory of the Genesis Effect -- a tale of paired emergence that just might echo the deepest truth in all biology: life begins in twos.

"Maybe Earth, too, matured – like a mother who had brought forth all she ever would."

— *A reflection on planetary life cycles and the mystery of origin*

Chapter 6: Noah's Ark as Symbol - The Silence of New Creations

Throughout this book, we've explored the idea that humanity – and indeed all life – may have originated not from a single ancestral chain, but from multiple, independent genesis events. A parallel emergence of pairs. And in that sense, one of the most enduring biblical stories ever told may carry a deeper message than we've ever realized.

The story of Noah's Ark is among the most famous in all of biblical scripture. It tells of a righteous man, a divine warning, a great flood, and a vessel built to preserve life. According to the account, two of every animal, male and female, were brought aboard. When the waters subsided, they were released to repopulate the world. The imagery is powerful. The symbolism, perhaps, even more so.

Traditionally, this story has been interpreted as one of obedience, judgment, and divine rescue. But let's consider an alternate reading, or interpretation: What if Noah's Ark isn't just about preservation, but is also about pattern? What if it doesn't just reflect a restart of life, but likewise reflects a kind of mirror for how life began in the first place?

In that light, the Ark becomes not a boat, but a *biological metaphor* of sorts. The pairs of animals are not *passengers* to view this metaphor, but instead are prototypes. The flood isn't a flood in any literal sense and instead is a symbolic reference pointing to a vast void, or of the *pre-life chaos* – in short representing the biological *zero point* before chaos gives way to order and uniformity. And Noah isn't just a man, he's a symbol of genesis itself. The life bringer. The divider of species. The keeper of boundaries.

If life began with single pairs emerging from Earth in different regions – each under its own genesis effect – then the Ark may represent an ancient, encoded memory of that process. The myth captures a truth in symbolic form, which is that life moves forward by way of twos: a male and a female. A seed and a vessel. A unity that contains within it the potential for continuity and fruitfulness.

This interpretation does not seek to disprove the suggested spiritual ideology of the story. In fact, it preserves it by revealing that the sacred and the symbolic are not enemies, but instead are allies. That the Bible, like many ancient texts, may speak a truth deeper than science – if only we are willing to consider it as mythically encoded history.

The story of the Ark then becomes the final echo in this book's central theory: It doesn't need to be fact to be real. It doesn't need to be literal to be true. What matters is the shape of the story – it's dimensions – and where that shape matches the *genesis pattern* we've explored from every other angle.

Perhaps that's why this story survived at all – because it remembered something we forgot: That life, in its origin, always comes two by two. And maybe we're all still sailing that Ark together – paired by time, moving through the flood of history.

— ✧ —

The Ark seen not merely as a vessel of survival, but as a metaphorical symbol of life's mysterious inception or beginning.

"If language is the fingerprint of origin, then Mandarin speaks for the first voice of our kind."

— *from Adam and Eve Were Chinese*

Chapter 7: Language vs. Nation - Rethinking Human Diversity

What defines a people? Is it a flag? A government? A shared border? Or is it something more fundamental, more primal – like a shared tongue?

Throughout this book, we've used modern geopolitical nationalities to illustrate the concept of population dominance and demographic origin. We've accepted the ISO-standard list of 249 countries and territories as a lens through which to view the human story. It's an imperfect lens, but a practical one.

But what if there's another lens? One older than maps, deeper than constitutions, and less transient than political regimes?

As of today, there are an estimated 7,847 recognized languages in the world depending on who you ask, since some estimates put it closer to the 7,100-to-7,200 range. It's a whole lot of languages in any case. But for the purposes of this book – and to simply the math – let's just round it down to 7,000 in total.

Some of these languages are spoken by billions, others by only a few dozen people, which is also according to the ISO. Then some are preserved in writing while others exist only in oral tradition. But each language represents a distinct cognitive universe – a unique structure of thought, sound, and culture. And unlike modern countries, most languages evolved organically – over time – from the ground up.

A worthwhile point to make, however, is that creating and perfecting a practical and usable language is a daunting task. The culmination of language creation – and by extension adoption – doesn't happen quickly. Indeed, such adoption would arguably take many, many years of refinement to reach even a reasonable level of *linguistic perfection* you might say. And spoken language is nothing to say of written language, because once you get into *written language* then things instantly become much more complicated compared to only spoken words.

One example of a man who attempted to create his own unique language, but ultimately gave up, was with John Wilkins (1614-1672). Wilkins was a 17th-century philosopher and cleric who sought to create a *philosophical language* that could express all human knowledge, or a kind of universal logic.

He spent decades working to perfect his language, but abandoned it in the end. As it turned out, the complexity of what he hoped to standardize, being a language that could be both cohesive and universally functional, proved impossible for any one man to perfect. And so that was the end of that experiment for one lone man trying to create a fully functional language.

So here's the question:

If each language represents a unique worldview, might it also represent a unique origin?

While countries rise and fall, and borders shift with the tides of history, languages have been among the most resilient carriers of identity. They encode not just communication, but culture, memory and ancestral lineage. In this sense, language may be a more accurate way to track human diversity than flags or political boundaries – or even our expressed understanding of genetics, which may be faulty.

Consider this: If there are at least 7,000 distinct languages, is it possible that there were also thousands of distinct *Genesis Effects*?

Independent origin points? Unique pairs of early humans who developed separately but simultaneously across different environments, climates, and contexts? These separate and distinct peoples presumably would have also created, or evolved, their own respectively distinct languages, or tongues.

To return to an earlier metaphor: *"If humanity is a species like any other, then perhaps we are best understood not as a single line of descent, but as a tree with many branches."* And consider that each language is most likely a branch – a visible, audible record of where that limb has grown.

This framing also casts new light on the Mandarin-speaking Chinese population, the largest single linguistic group in the world. Because if each language reflects a unique "breed" of humanity, indeed a separate Genesis pair, then the extraordinary scale of the Chinese population is statistically profound. It suggests that either the Chinese were among the very first to emerge, or they were uniquely positioned for reproductive and cultural dominance. In either case, the math becomes increasingly unfavorable to the idea that another group came before them.

Indeed, it may be more than improbable, it may be mathematically impossible for any breed of human to have come before that of the Chinese.

So what defines a people?

The answer may lie not in a passport, nor a border. It may lie in the first word ever spoken in each tongue – the first shared sound between a new Adam and Eve pair.*

— ✧ —

(*For a full list of the 249 recognized nationalities referenced throughout this work, see the Appendix. (The 7,000+ languages are not listed here.)

If all humans came out of Africa, then this is basically what it would look like as far as a tree is concerned.

"Whoever came first, it is statistically improbable it could have been Africans — because if it were, then Mandarin would be their language. And it's not."

— *Reflective Observation on Linguistic Descent*

Reader Q&A: Common Questions and Objections

Q: If humans didn't originate in Africa, how do you explain the fossil and genetic evidence pointing there?

A: The presence of early human fossils and rich genetic diversity in Africa could reflect a major genesis event, but not necessarily the only one. My theory doesn't deny human emergence in Africa; it simply questions whether all human groups originated from that single event. Parallel genesis events across other regions, including East Asia, may have occurred independently and left fewer fossil traces due to time, terrain, or degradation.

Q: Why aren't new human nationalities or species forming today?

A: Just as individual life forms stop growing upon reaching maturity, the Earth's ecosystem may have passed its own phase of spontaneous biological genesis. Once the global biosphere stabilized with sustainable reproduction across existing species, the conditions necessary for entirely new formations may have simply faded out of existence.

Q: Doesn't all this sound like pseudoscience?

A: It's not pseudoscience. It's a hypothesis grounded in logic, population statistics, comparative biology, and even mathematics. I make no supernatural claims; and I invite readers to challenge the ideas thoughtfully. Just because an idea questions consensus doesn't make it false. Scientific history is full of once-dismissed theories that later proved revolutionary.

A: I don't reject evolution. I reinterpret the origin points. Evolution still explains adaptation, diversification, and inheritance within species. But the question of how those species, or nationalities, first emerged remains open to discovery. I propose a framework that supports multiple, environment-specific emergences rather than one universal tree.

Q: Why emphasize China in particular?

A: Statistically, China holds the largest and most enduring population on Earth. Its cultural continuity and civilizational age make it a compelling candidate for early human emergence. While this idea may challenge mainstream views, it's based on observable demographic dominance and historical stability, not cultural favoritism.

Q: Doesn't this undermine religious interpretations of creation?

A: Not at all. In fact, this theory may harmonize with certain religious symbols and texts, like the story of Adam and Eve or Noah's Ark. These stories may preserve ancient truths encoded in mythic language. Science and symbolism can complement each other when viewed through the lens of pattern and metaphor.

Q: Isn't it possible that all human variation, as in skin color, body shape, facial features, etc., came from a single ancestral group that migrated out of Africa over tens of thousands of years?

A: That's the mainstream view, but when we examine it critically, it presents a striking problem: You don't see this level of divergence anywhere else in nature over so few generations. No known species has produced the kind of extreme anatomical, cultural, and genetic variation that modern humans exhibit – not from a single lineage, and not in such a short evolutionary window.

You might find variation within a species (dog breeds, for example), but those changes are typically either minor or artificially selected. What we see in humanity is global, distinct, and complex, spanning from limb proportions to eye structure, from hair type to skin tone, from skull shape to vocal qualities, and more.

So it raises the question: *"Where is the biological precedent?"* If we can't find it in other species, then perhaps another explanation, such as the *Genesis Effect*, is worth serious consideration.

Q: Isn't it more likely that different populations emerged in parallel? That different nationalities, or 'breeds' of humans, came into being separately?

A: That's the core theory explored in this book. Instead of assuming a single human origin point, it considers the possibility that humanity emerged through multiple parallel genesis events, or separate *Adam and Eve pairs* so to speak. The vast differences in linguistic, anatomical, and cultural traits suggest not just branching, but separate roots. This theory doesn't claim to replace the Out-of-Africa model, it simply suggests an alternate, perhaps complementary, lens.

Q: What about the idea that modern science has proven that all humans share 99.9% of the same DNA? Doesn't that prove we all came from the same source?

A: This is a common and compelling argument. But genetic similarity doesn't always imply a shared point of origin, as it can also indicate shared biological constraints. All mammals, for instance, share huge portions of DNA. Even humans and chimpanzees share ~98.8% of their genetic code. And yet, no one confuses the two. A high percentage of shared DNA can also result from evolutionary convergence or parallel design. The 0.1% that's different in human beings accounts for everything from eye shape to immune responses, and from skin tone to metabolism. Small differences can produce massive observable diversity.

Q: You've argued that the Chinese may have come first. But isn't it more accurate to say we can't really know who came first?

A: Yes, and that's the nuanced position this book ultimately lands on. The thesis isn't that *"we know for sure."* It's that the numbers suggest a **very** high likelihood that the Chinese were first if we base our logic on present-day population dominance, linguistic resilience, and civilizational continuity. But no one can prove the exact order of emergence. That's why this book offers a mathematical and philosophical framework, not a declaration of absolute truth.

Q: Isn't the idea that Africans gave rise to all other nationalities a widely accepted consensus?

A: It is. But consensus isn't the same thing as certainty. Scientific consensus is often revised. At one point, it was the consensus that ulcers were caused by stress, which was abandoned when we discovered the *Helicobacter pylori* strain of bacteria. Similarly, the consensus that all continents were fixed in place was overturned by the discovery of *plate tectonics*, which is relative to movement of the Earth's mantle . In contrast, the Out-of-Africa model is supported by genetic and archaeological evidence. However, much of that evidence is not only circumstantial, but it often fails to explain the radical differences in physiology, language, and culture that emerged in humans over arguably extremely short time spans.

Q: Has anything like this kind of divergence happened elsewhere in the animal kingdom?

A: Not to the same degree. We do see what's called *speciation*, which is where one species branches into multiple species, but those changes are usually subtle over extremely long time spans, as in hundreds of thousands or millions of years. You don't get radically different canines from a single ancestor in 40,000 years, for instance. And you definitely don't get language systems emerging rapidly. Human language is extraordinarily complex. And if anything, the comparison of humans to animal breeds supports the idea of separate origin points rather than a single root. In that way, you don't get a tiger, a lion, and a housecat all from the same prototype in a few millennia. So why assume that humans, who are even more differentiated, came from a single pair?

Q: Hasn't the Chinese language, specifically Mandarin, been in continuous use for thousands of years?

A: Yes, and that's part of what makes Mandarin such a compelling case study. It's not merely the most spoken language today, but it's one of the oldest documented linguistic traditions still in use. When we ask which language shows the greatest durability and continuity, Mandarin rises to the top. That continuity may not be coincidental. It might signal something deeper, like linguistic priority, or even evolutionary primacy.

Q: How likely is it, mathematically speaking, that Mandarin could have simply been the first language by random chance?

A: Let's look at it statistically. If we assume there are approximately 7,000 distinct human languages, and each had an equal chance of being the first to emerge, the probability that Mandarin was the first would be:

$$P(\text{Mandarin as first}) = 1 / 7000 \approx 0.00014 \text{ or } 0.014\%$$

That's a 1 in 7,000 chance – essentially zero. And yet, Mandarin is the most spoken, most historically preserved, and most deeply rooted language on Earth.

This leads to a compelling question:

If Mandarin wasn't the first, why does it look so much like it was?

Statistically speaking, such global dominance from a randomly placed origin point is extremely unlikely. That doesn't prove

Mandarin came first, but it casts doubt on the idea that it arose late or purely by chance.

****

[1] **Note:** While every effort was made to preserve the integrity of this manuscript, one mathematically significant equation did inexplicably vanish during the editing process. No technical cause was found. The author would like to thank the probable ghost of *John Wilkins* for inspiring a more elegant revision (the part in white up there), and for reminding us that not all lost knowledge stays lost forever!

— ✧ —

Visual Comparison of Human Origin Models

This section provides a side-by-side visual representation of the two dominant models of human origin: the mainstream Out-of-Africa theory and the alternative Genesis Effect hypothesis. These illustrations offer a simplified conceptual overview, not detailed anthropological mappings. However, they help clarify the fundamental difference between a single-point origin versus multiple parallel emergence events.

Figure 1: Mainstream Out-of-Africa Model — One geographic origin radiating outward over time.

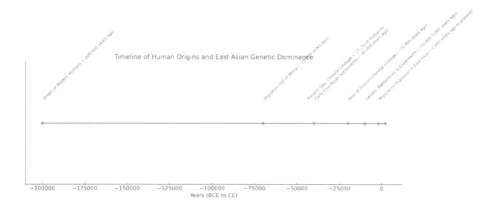

Figure 2: Genesis Effect Model — Multiple distinct genesis events occurring independently across regions.

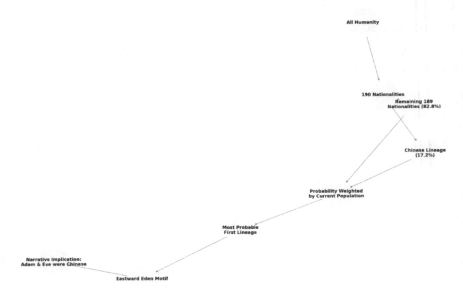

Graphical Probability Tree: Adam & Eve as the First Chinese Humans

All Humanity

190 Nationalities
Remaining 189
Nationalities (82.8%)

Chinese Lineage
(17.2%)

Probability Weighted
by Current Population

Most Probable
First Lineage

Narrative Implication:
Adam & Eve were Chinese

Eastward Eden Motif

Conclusion

In stepping back from the statistical branches, symbolic stories, and ancestral maps we've considered, this book arrives not at a definitive answer, but at a powerful possibility: Could it be that humanity's origin story has more than one root? That the Genesis Effect, as proposed herein, offers a lens through which we might interpret both ancient myths and observable demographic realities without contradiction?

While the Out-of-Africa model remains a cornerstone of mainstream science, it does not invalidate the concept that multiple genesis events could have occurred independently, shaped by the unique geochemical and atmospheric conditions of various regions. The notion that Homo sapiens may have formed from the *'dust of the Earth'* not once, but many times – and in parallel across the planet – is radical only if we assume that nature prefers simplicity to abundance.

And if that's true – not just biologically but cosmically – then each distinct nationality, population, or even unique linguistic community, may reflect not a divergence from a singular ancestor, but a separate dawn all its own. In this framing, China's vast and enduring civilization may be seen not merely as populous, but primordial.

Of course, we may never prove this theory in a laboratory, nor extract it from fossil beds with absolute clarity. But not all truths are discovered through excavation: some are revealed through synthesis, some through symmetry, and some through math.

Whether or not the reader accepts the *Genesis Effect* described herein as literal, symbolic, or simply provocative, the purpose of this book has always been to stretch the boundaries of accepted thought. If it succeeded in doing that, even briefly, then it fulfilled its purpose.

Perhaps the greatest question we can ask at this stage of human reflection is not *where did we come from?*, but *are we still emerging?* And if so, what stories will our future ancestors tell about us?

"Some conclusions live not in the words we write, but in the spaces we leave unwritten."

— From the Unwritten Pages

The author unseen, the story unwritten.

Final Reflections from the Author

"There isn't any one thing in the universe that knows everything there is to know about the universe. And so the universe remains a mystery even unto itself."

— James Shepard

• Truth may wear a lab coat or a crown—but never both at once.

• The more certain we are, the less room we leave for revelation.

• Even math has mysteries it cannot solve.

• Faith is the bridge between what we know and what we need to believe.

- The stars don't explain themselves. We do that for them.

- Nothing stays true longer than the questions we never stop asking.

- If nature made us, then nature made our doubt, too.

- In every myth, there's a math problem waiting to be solved.

- Some truths are too large to live inside one story.

- The universe isn't obligated to make sense – but we are compelled to try.

- Even the dust we came from has a past we don't understand.

- To be human is to inherit mystery we did not choose.

- Maybe the Garden wasn't lost – it just kept growing in directions we stopped looking.

"The first word ever spoken in each tongue may mark the birthplace of an entire people."

— *from Chapter 7: Language vs. Nation*

Appendix

On the Use of the Term "Genesis Effect"
The term *Genesis Effect*, as used throughout this book, refers to the idea that certain life forms – particularly Homo sapiens – may have emerged independently in multiple regions around the world, rather than from a single common ancestor. This concept proposes that life may form in discrete pairings under specific environmental and energetic conditions, much like mold forms on the surface of tomato soup: not through migration, but through recurrence.

Note on Species Pairings
While this book focuses on human origins, the same principle could apply to other species – canines, felines, reptiles, birds, even plant life. If environmental conditions support the spontaneous emergence of one life form, they may support many, each appearing as male–female or seed–spore pairings. This is what I refer to as the Genesis Effect, scaled across the biosphere.

Reconsidering the Adam & Eve Framework
In this context, the biblical story of Adam and Eve is not approached as a religious truth, but as a symbolic or metaphorical encoding of a natural process. Each "Adam and Eve" pair may represent the first viable instance of a self-replicating species in a given region. This notion supports – not contradicts – the scientific principle of environmental influence on biology.

The Role of Myth in Science
Ancient stories often contain symbols that were once tethered to real observations. Noah's Ark, for example, may represent the memory of a bottleneck event or even an intuitive allegory for

paired emergence – two of every kind. This does not mean the literal stories are true, but that they may have symbolic relevance when interpreted through a different lens.

Final Acknowledgment of Scientific Boundaries

Nothing in this book is meant to replace the scientific method. Rather, it is meant to ask questions that science may not yet be able to answer. The ideas presented here are exploratory – rooted in demographic evidence, evolutionary logic, symbolic patterns, and a respect for mystery. If the universe has more than one story to tell, then we should be listening for more than one language.

Further Reading & Related Theories

- Gaia Hypothesis Overview:

https://www.sciencedirect.com/topics/earth-and-planetary-sciences/gaia-hypothesis

- Philosophical Perspectives on Gaia:

https://academic.oup.com/bioscience/article/64/5/455/2754268

- Gaia Hypothesis - Wikipedia:

https://en.wikipedia.org/wiki/Gaia_hypothesis

- Gaia Hypothesis - Harvard University:

https://courses.seas.harvard.edu/climate/eli/Courses/EPS281r/Sources/Gaia/Gaia-hypothesis-wikipedia.pdf

- Resurrecting Gaia: Harnessing the Free Energy Principle:

https://pmc.ncbi.nlm.nih.gov/articles/PMC10322209/

Recognized Nationalities of the World

The list of 249 countries that follows represents widely recognized nations and territories from across the globe, each symbolizing a distinct nationality under modern geopolitical classification. While the term "nationality" may carry legal, ethnic, or cultural implications depending on context, it is used here to denote the diversity of the human species as acknowledged through the ISO 3166 international standard. In keeping with the themes of this book, these nationalities may be viewed not merely as political constructs, but as potential reflections of the many evolutionary threads — or Genesis Effects — that have shaped Homo sapiens across time and geography...

A

- Afghanistan
- Albania
- Algeria
- American Samoa
- Andorra
- Angola
- Anguilla
- Antarctica
- Antigua and Barbuda
- Argentina
- Armenia
- Aruba
- Australia
- Austria
- Azerbaijan

B

- Bahamas
- Bahrain
- Bangladesh
- Barbados
- Belarus
- Belgium
- Belize
- Benin
- Bermuda
- Bhutan
- Bolivia, Plurinational State of
- Bonaire, Sint Eustatius and Saba
- Bosnia and Herzegovina
- Botswana
- Bouvet Island
- Brazil
- British Indian Ocean Territory
- Brunei Darussalam
- Bulgaria
- Burkina Faso
- Burundi

C

- Cabo Verde
- Cambodia
- Cameroon
- Canada
- Cayman Islands
- Central African Republic
- Chad
- Chile
- China

- Christmas Island
- Cocos (Keeling) Islands
- Colombia
- Comoros
- Congo
- Congo, The Democratic Republic of the
- Cook Islands
- Costa Rica
- Croatia
- Cuba
- Curaçao
- Cyprus
- Czechia
- Côte d'Ivoire

D

- Denmark
- Djibouti
- Dominica
- Dominican Republic

E

- Ecuador
- Egypt
- El Salvador
- Equatorial Guinea
- Eritrea
- Estonia
- Eswatini
- Ethiopia

F

- Falkland Islands (Malvinas)
- Faroe Islands

- Fiji
- Finland
- France
- French Guiana
- French Polynesia
- French Southern Territories

G

- Gabon
- Gambia
- Georgia
- Germany
- Ghana
- Gibraltar
- Greece
- Greenland
- Grenada
- Guadeloupe
- Guam
- Guatemala
- Guernsey
- Guinea
- Guinea-Bissau
- Guyana

H

- Haiti
- Heard Island and McDonald Islands
- Holy See (Vatican City State)
- Honduras
- Hong Kong
- Hungary

I

- Iceland
- India
- Indonesia
- Iran, Islamic Republic of
- Iraq
- Ireland
- Isle of Man
- Israel
- Italy

J

- Jamaica
- Japan
- Jersey
- Jordan

K

- Kazakhstan
- Kenya
- Kiribati
- Korea, Democratic People's Republic of
- Korea, Republic of
- Kuwait
- Kyrgyzstan

L

- Lao People's Democratic Republic
- Latvia
- Lebanon
- Lesotho
- Liberia
- Libya
- Liechtenstein
- Lithuania

- Luxembourg

M

- Macao
- Madagascar
- Malawi
- Malaysia
- Maldives
- Mali
- Malta
- Marshall Islands
- Martinique
- Mauritania
- Mauritius
- Mayotte
- Mexico
- Micronesia, Federated States of
- Moldova, Republic of
- Monaco
- Mongolia
- Montenegro
- Montserrat
- Morocco
- Mozambique
- Myanmar

N

- Namibia
- Nauru
- Nepal
- Netherlands
- New Caledonia
- New Zealand

- Nicaragua
- Niger
- Nigeria
- Niue
- Norfolk Island
- North Macedonia
- Northern Mariana Islands
- Norway

O

- Oman

P

- Pakistan
- Palau
- Palestine, State of
- Panama
- Papua New Guinea
- Paraguay
- Peru
- Philippines
- Pitcairn
- Poland
- Portugal
- Puerto Rico

Q

- Qatar

R

- Romania
- Russian Federation

- Rwanda
- Réunion

S

- Saint Barthélemy
- Saint Helena, Ascension and Tristan da Cunha
- Saint Kitts and Nevis
- Saint Lucia
- Saint Martin (French part)
- Saint Pierre and Miquelon
- Saint Vincent and the Grenadines
- Samoa
- San Marino
- Sao Tome and Principe
- Saudi Arabia
- Senegal
- Serbia
- Seychelles
- Sierra Leone
- Singapore
- Sint Maarten (Dutch part)
- Slovakia
- Slovenia
- Solomon Islands
- Somalia
- South Africa
- South Georgia and the South Sandwich Islands
- South Sudan
- Spain
- Sri Lanka
- Sudan
- Suriname
- Svalbard and Jan Mayen

- Sweden
- Switzerland
- Syrian Arab Republic

T

- Taiwan, Province of China
- Tajikistan
- Tanzania, United Republic of
- Thailand
- Timor-Leste
- Togo
- Tokelau
- Tonga
- Trinidad and Tobago
- Tunisia
- Turkey
- Turkmenistan
- Turks and Caicos Islands
- Tuvalu

U

- Uganda
- Ukraine
- United Arab Emirates
- United Kingdom
- United States
- United States Minor Outlying Islands
- Uruguay
- Uzbekistan

V

- Vanuatu
- Venezuela, Bolivarian Republic of
- Viet Nam

- Virgin Islands, British
- Virgin Islands, U.S.

- Wallis and Futuna
- Western Sahara

- Yemen

- Zambia & Zimbabwe

— ✧ —

Noah's Ark symbolic of anchoring at the Great Wall of China, not somewhere in Africa.

Epilogue – Voices They Tried to Silence

Ecclesiastes and Enoch in the Shadow of the Genesis Effect

The Skeptic from the Inside (Ecclesiastes)

The Book of Ecclesiastes, traditionally attributed to King Solomon, reads more like philosophical poetry than religious doctrine. It is skeptical, poetic, and restless – a book that refuses to draw hard lines around truth or understanding. This same tone, of observing mystery without attempting to tame it, lies at the heart of the Genesis Effect theory.

Consider Ecclesiastes 1:4–7:

"Generations come and generations go, but the earth remains forever. The sun rises and the sun sets, and hurries back to where it rises. The wind blows to the south and turns to the north; round and round it goes, ever returning on its course. All streams flow into the sea, yet the sea is never full."

This view of nature's unbroken cycle reflects the idea that life may not have begun once and migrated outward, but instead may arise again and again, just as rivers endlessly return to the sea.

Ecclesiastes 3:11 deepens this awe:

"He has made everything beautiful in its time. He has also set eternity in the human heart; yet no one can fathom what God has done from beginning to end."

Here, mystery is sacred. Knowledge is partial. These verses align more closely with open-ended scientific and philosophical inquiry than with dogma.

The Prophet from the Outside (Enoch)

The Book of Enoch, once widely known but later banned from most biblical canons, presents a radically different voice, one that is cosmic, apocalyptic, and startlingly visionary. It speaks of 'Watchers' – divine beings who descend to Earth and interfere with the natural order.

Enoch 6:1–2 reads:

"And it came to pass... that the sons of heaven saw the daughters of men that they were beautiful; and they took for themselves wives of all whom they chose."

In symbolic terms, this could be seen as a mythological explanation for sudden shifts or enhancements in the human condition – whether biological, spiritual, or both. The fact that Enoch was banned lends weight to its disruptive potential. It doesn't contradict science directly, but it points to a more ancient and unsettling question: *What if our origin story was interfered with, altered, or accelerated?*

Whether literal or allegorical, the Book of Enoch invites us to consider that life on Earth may have unfolded in ways we do not fully understand – and that some knowledge has been purposely obscured.

Together, Ecclesiastes and Enoch embody the two outer limits of ancient thought: one skeptical, grounded, and cyclical; the other visionary, hidden, and nearly erased. One survived by royal protection. The other was banished by theological gatekeepers.

Yet both speak to a shared reverence for mystery. And in that reverence, we find a quiet affirmation of the Genesis Effect – a theory that does not claim to know, but dares to wonder.

Perhaps these books were not meant to explain our origin, but to remind us that no one truly can.

And so we return to the core insight:

"There isn't any one thing in the universe that knows everything there is to know about the universe. And so the universe remains a mystery even unto itself." – James Shepard

Acknowledgments

This book was not written in isolation – nor could it have been. The journey of putting these thoughts to paper has been shaped by countless influences, seen and unseen, known and unknown.

To those thinkers, scientists, philosophers, and storytellers throughout history who dared to challenge consensus and question the narratives handed down to them, I owe you a debt of intellectual courage and gratitude. You paved the way for voices like mine to wonder aloud.

To my close friends and companions, as well as my family members, who have endured countless hours of me rambling about theories that skirt the edge of science and speculation, you know who you are. Thank you for listening, questioning, and offering your honesty.

To every reader willing to approach this book with an open mind and a curious heart, thank you. Your willingness to sit with uncomfortable questions and entertain alternate frameworks of thought is what gives this work its true meaning.

And finally, to the quiet hours, the sleepless nights, and the stubborn need to understand something deeper, I acknowledge you not as burdens, but as blessings. For without them, this book would never have existed.

Here's to the unknown, and to all who chase it. Best wishes...

— ✧ —

Just two old men left to ponder their reality along the never-ending path of Creation...

About the Author

James Shepard is a lifelong thinker, investigator, and truth-seeker who isn't afraid to challenge the mainstream narrative – especially when the math doesn't add up, and the patterns whisper a deeper story. With a mind rooted in logic, but a spirit stirred by philosophy, he blends the rational and the intuitive to ask the kinds of questions most people are too afraid to ask; and dares to offer answers most people never see coming.

Born with an innate curiosity for origins – of life, of ideas, of everything – he has spent decades exploring the hidden intersections between biology, cosmology, language, myth, and mathematics. He believes the truth is often buried beneath layers of assumption, and that sometimes the oldest stories carry the most revolutionary insights... if you know how to read them.

A self-educated polymath and unapologetic rebel against intellectual conformity, the author writes not to preach answers, but to spark new questions – the kind that can rearrange your understanding of the world in just a few pages.

This book, like the mind that birthed it, is a fusion of science and soul. If it made you pause, question, or argue – then it's done its job.

"The truth of our origin may not lie in the first man, but in the first moment another voice broke his silence — and it was the woman."

— *from ADAM AND EVE WERE CHINESE*